What Matters Most

Deuteronomy 6 in 3D

An ancient plan for modern parents

BY GARNETT REID

randall house

114 Bush Rd | Nashville, TN 37217

randallhouse.com

Deuteronomy 6 in 3D

Published by Randall House Publications
114 Bush Road
Nashville, TN 37217

Printed in the United States of America

13-ISBN 9780892656264

table of contents

D6 DOWNLOAD: THE TEXT—
What Deuteronomy 6 means in context 7

D6 DNA: THE THREAD—
Where Deuteronomy 6 leads in scripture 33

D6 DYNAMICS: THE TEACHING—
How Deuteronomy 6 looks in life 43

Ready for the unimaginable

Glioma. Cancer. A brain tumor. That diagnosis explained our otherwise healthy 26-year-old son Seth's sudden seizures. Our world convulsed. Carol and I had always rejoiced that Seth had come to trust Christ years before. We were confident from watching his life over those two-and-a-half decades that he knew how to live with faith in his Lord. Now, though, came the suddenly relevant question no parent wants to ever face: had we helped him get ready to die with the same faith?

In a very real sense, D6 parenting should prepare our children to die. If we succeed at that, we will have prepared them to live.

Successful surgery removed Seth's tumor with no follow-up radiation or chemotherapy needed. He is now married and teaching fourth grade a year-and-a-half past the diagnosis. His mother and I are still amazed that not only has God chosen to spare his life, but also to empower his growth in spiritual maturity and Christlikeness. In fact, we are doubly blessed to have two sons living for God.

More than any other book in the Old Testament, Deuteronomy gets the ball rolling by helping us understand what living for God really looks like. This fifth book of Moses is a pivot book; it looks back at how God chose and redeemed His people and sets its sights ahead toward all that He has promised them.

Its influence pervades the rest of the Bible as well. The history books of the Old Testament unfold its themes in the real-life setting of the covenant community. Old Covenant prophets used Deuteronomy as the basis for many of their oracles. In its pages we catch the first formal glimpse of the New Covenant and of that "Prophet," Christ, who would come as its mediator. The book itself comes to us as both a sermon and a covenant. As a sermon, it invites us to believe God. As a covenant, it calls us to love God.

Chapter 6 may offer the most vital message of the book to 21st century parents. Here Moses prioritizes life under the most essential relationship of all: loving God more than anything else. Then he explains how that relationship can keep on going forever: loving your children so much that they, too, love God more than anything else.

Moses prioritizes life under the most essential relationship of all: loving God more than anything else.

Own these words! They tell what matters most. All that's at stake is your life and the lives of those you love the most.

D6 DOWNLOAD: THE TEXT

What Deuteronomy 6 means in context

It's not very cool these days to talk about "the most important thing in life," the meaning of everything, or those kinds of vague, touchy, mind-game questions. Such subjects don't make for tight, 90-second sound bites. Plus we're told they're not practical, they divide people, they can be messy, etc.

The problem is that when we download songs, swipe the debit card, hang out with friends, vote for a candidate, plan the family trip to the beach, surf the web, take the kids to soccer practice, fret over a CT scan—when we just live our lives, that is—we live by priorities which reflect things that *do* matter to us, things that give life meaning.

Only a relationship with God can center our lives on any meaning that satisfies. With Him as the axis, the hub, everything else stays in balance. The margins connect; all the "stuff" means something because it all comes back to Him and us on a person-to-person level. The Bible is all about that relationship and how it can happen.

Imagine the Bible portraying that relationship as a mouth-watering pie, whatever your favorite kind may be. Deuteronomy 6 slides a slice of that pie across the table and invites you to try a bite. And if we have one taste and see that "the Lord is good," we'll want to eat the whole pie. Your D6 slice, appropriately, has six bites. Here's the first one.

1. WE EXAMINE THE RELATIONSHIP:

The nexus of life itself is experiencing the fear of God (Deuteronomy 6:1-3)

> *Now this is the commandment, the statutes and the rules that the Lord your God commanded me to teach you, that you may do them in the land to which you are going over, to possess it, that you may fear the Lord your God, you and your son and your son's son, by keeping all his statutes and his commandments, which I command you, all the days of your life, and that your days may be long. Hear therefore, O Israel, and be careful to do them, that it may go well with you, and that you may multiply greatly, as the Lord, the God of your fathers, has promised you, in a land flowing with milk and honey.*

Down deep in the core of who we are is a massive empty spot that nothing can fill except God. According to the Old Testament, the only way that spot can be filled is to fear Him.

That's how the first part of the Bible describes the relationship—fearing God—and that's Moses' main concern in Deuteronomy 6.

Why All the Fuss?
The importance of the relationship

Verses 1-3 join Deuteronomy 5:22-33 to link two of the Old Testament's greatest teaching points about God. At their heart, both the Ten Commandments (5:6-21) and the *Shema* (6:4-9) press home one main idea: God demands and deserves first place in our lives. So these three verses opening chapter 6 are ***focal*** in making God's preeminence clear to us. Notice carefully that verse 1 speaks not of "commandments" plural, but of "*the* commandment." That's what 5:31 has just said, too. Everything that follows in chapter 6 is one great truth, a ***single***, holistic principle that embraces all of life. We're dealing, then, with one command, really. Note, too, that this relationship explained in Deuteronomy 6 is ***binding***. It is, after all, a commandment. It's an imperative, a must. If we reject it, we're in real trouble.

> God just loves to get down into the cracks and crevices where we spend our seconds and minutes and hours so that even those details reflect His good plan for us.

Although it is a single truth, this relationship with God touches every part of life, as suggested by those plural nouns that give shape and texture to the singular commandment—

the "statutes" and "rules." God just loves to get down into the cracks and crevices where we spend our seconds and minutes and hours so that even those details reflect His good plan for us. Clearly the relationship is ***comprehensive*** as well.

So important is our relationship with God that He makes a way for others to hear about it. Therefore it is ***communicable***; we must pass it along, as the chapter will stress later. "The LORD your God commanded me to *teach* you," verse 1 notes. From God to Moses to the people, the word spreads that everybody needs to know the Lord. It's as if this sets a sequence in motion that will soon become critical to the strategy of Deuteronomy 6: parent to children to children's children.

"Knowing" God means obeying Him, though. The Lord wants His people "to do" those things which will show they really do know Him. The relationship is therefore ***behavioral***. We must "live" God as we go about living life. And we must do it in place: "in the land," Moses tells the people. For us, that means our relationship with God must be ***grounded*** in real life. In all of those familiar settings that map our lives, the fact that *we know God* must say more about us than anything else.

In all of those familiar settings that map our lives, the fact that we know God must say more about us than anything else.

What's It All About?

The essence of the relationship

All that Moses said in verse 1 points to the great purpose which opens verse 2: "that you may fear the LORD your God." This fear of the Lord stands at the beginning (v. 2), middle (v. 13), and end (v. 24) of Deuteronomy six. The Old Testament uses this phrase so often—over 130 times—that it comes to be the common way of describing a relationship with God. It is the glue that holds the covenant community together. What "being born again" is to New Testament believers "fearing God" is to Old Testament people of faith.

We should unpack this concept of "fear," though, so that we don't get the wrong impression of what the phrase means. While at first it does indeed suggest a sense of dread and alarm before a holy God, it moves along a continuum leading to awe and reverence, then finally to trust and worship. Notice that fear is coupled with love in Deuteronomy 10:12 so that the two become virtually the same thing. The "fear of the LORD" is conviction and repentance and deliverance and joy and peace all rolled into one. It is a relationship with God packaged in a phrase we can grasp.

While we cannot force others to embrace the relationship, *we can teach the fear of the Lord* (Psalm 34:11). We can—and we must—instruct our children in its content, model its effect before them, and urge them to commit their lives to it. Our four-year-old granddaughter Katherine made it clear her taste was not disposed to enjoy macaroni and cheese even though it's a favorite with most preschoolers. So in our attempt to change that disposition, we set her place at the table with her princess dishes, surrounded her serving of macaroni with her favorite foods, raved to her about how good macaroni is, pointed out that her sister Allison loves it, and that ice cream would be the next course on the menu if she'd eat her mac and cheese. She finally gave in—and liked it! When our children and those closest to us see how satisfying the fear of the Lord really is and hear the truth about it, some of them will decide to try it. And they will like it.

When our children and those closest to us see how satisfying the fear of the Lord really is and hear the truth about it, some of them will decide to try it. And they will like it.

What's in It for Me?
The benefits of the relationship

The last part of verse 2 blends with verse 3 to convince us that a covenant relationship with God offers life at its best—the optimal life, the only life.

It Transcends Time

Moses reminds us that the fear of the Lord can travel from generation to generation, from your son to your son's son. Don't forget that God shows covenant love to thousands of generations of those who love Him and keep covenant loyalty (Deuteronomy 5:10).

It Saturates Life

We see again in verse 2 that submitting our heart and will to the Lord's statutes and commandments means we choose to please Him in every part of our lives. This is not just rule-keeping, but God-living—the kind of life that is never just a duty but a delight.

It Fills Every Day

Another benefit of knowing God is that the relationship stays constant on good days and bad alike—"all the days," as verse 2 puts it. The qualifier, "that your days may be long" is not a lock-down guarantee of extended physical life. No, lengthened days suggest the hope of experiencing more of God's blessings. It's like God expects us to say, "I want more of this!" So He gives it to us. It's a "long" time because it's such a good time because we are in this covenant with the Lord.

It's like God expects us to say, "I want more of this!" So He gives it to us.

It Grows Out of Loyalty

When the Lord commands us to "hear," He means for us to receive what He says, process it, believe it, and act on it. Loyalty to the covenant is not just trusting His Word, it is also "being careful to do it," as verse 3 says. We obey with intent and precision, and when we do, it will "go well with" us. The Hebrew expression is, "it will be good for us." The word translated "well" or "good" speaks of every blessing that satisfies God's people when they are in a covenant relationship with Him. It's good to know the Lord!

It Gives Us Hope

God's promise that He will "multiply" His people to the max (verse 3) points back to His covenant with Abraham. We have good reason for hope because our covenant God keeps His Word.

It Takes the Best Care of Us

The last phrase in verse 3 describes the richest food—"milk and honey"—as a way of saying that the Lord satisfies His people with all that they need. Deuteronomy 8:7-10 goes even further, telling us that He lavishes abundant blessing upon those who know Him.

2. WE EMBRACE THE RELATIONSHIP:

The passion of life is delighting in the love of God (Deuteronomy 6:4-5)

> *Hear, O Israel: The Lord our God, the Lord is one. You shall love the Lord your God with all your heart and with all your soul and with all your might.*

Now the relationship deepens. The "fear of the Lord" summarizes all the features involved in our relationship with Him. Yet as we have seen, the one quality in the relationship which sets our devotion aflame is love. The 16 Hebrew words in Deuteronomy 6:4-5 burn with the deepest affections possible in life and light the way to a glimpse into the very character of our God. The second bite of the D6 pie savors the love of God.

Listen to and Learn God

"*Shema*"—this simple Hebrew command, "listen," opens verse 4 as it does verse 3 before it. Along with verse 5, these words form the most familiar confession in Judaism. Observant Jews still recite the *Shema* every morning and evening. These unparalleled words challenge us on two fronts. First, they reveal the most profound truth about the character of the transcendent Being who made everything. Yet they also challenge us, as beings made in His image, with the supreme loyalty in life: loving Him with all that we are.

Verse 4 sets the tone for all that follows in the chapter, so we need to look at it carefully. A literal translation of the Hebrew reads, "Hear, Israel: the LORD our God, the LORD is one." Some suggest that these words stress the unity of God, that He is one in essence. While He reveals Himself in three persons in the Trinity, He is singular in who He is, and thus has one mind and one will.

While the Bible certainly teaches this truth, there is a better way to look at Deuteronomy 6:4. First, notice the names of God. He is our "God," translating the Hebrew *Elohim*. This title speaks of God's power, God's greatness. We might say it is His generic name. "LORD," on the other hand, is His "personal" name, His name of covenant, His name known in relationship. Some versions translate this name as Yahweh—*YHWH* in Hebrew—while others simply render it "LORD" in all capital letters.

This God is Yahweh; He is "our God." We know Him through a covenant relationship He began out of His love for us. The fact that "Yahweh is one" probably teaches that He is the only God. He is unique. No one like Him exists. A similar statement in Zechariah 14:7-9 suggests this, as do parallel phrases in other ancient Near Eastern literature.

Don't miss the impact of what this verse claims. Only one absolutely powerful being exists in the universe, and we can know Him in a meaningful relationship. If this is true, life offers endless possibilities for anyone who will link up with this God. The question, then, is *how* we can know Him.

> Only one absolutely powerful being exists in the universe, and we can know Him in a meaningful relationship.

Love and Live God

The answer to the question, "How can we know God?" is love. It all begins with His love. We can only respond with love for Him because He has loved us. Perhaps no word in history has suffered more abuse at the hands of those who claim it than "love." In Deuteronomy love is not primarily an emotion or a feeling. God commands it. Covenant love is a total commitment of the whole person out of selfless devotion to a spouse in a relationship. Without it we would not reflect God's image. We could not know ourselves, and certainly we could not know God.

Therefore love for God embraces all that loyalty is: devotion, commitment, trust, affection, obedience, and worship.

It rises within us: "with all your heart." To the Hebrews, the heart was the sum total of the inner person—mind, will, and emotion. Love expresses itself with all the force of one's personality, "with all your soul," and consumes the lover, "with all your strength." All that love is wraps itself around one's heart and mind and passion to energize every part of life with intense affection. Who or what we love supremely becomes everything to us. For the one who loves God, nothing in life makes sense unless it is seen in light of this absolute devotion to Him. The primal reality in life is God and the primal relationship one of love for Him—"Love the LORD your God."

> Who or what we love supremely becomes everything to us.

3. WE NURTURE THE RELATIONSHIP:

The responsibility of life is shaping a generation for God (Deuteronomy 6:6-9)

> *And these words that I command you today shall be on your heart. You shall teach them diligently to your children, and shall talk of them when you sit in your house, and when you walk by the way, and when you lie down, and when you rise. You shall bind them as a sign on your hand, and they shall be as frontlets between your eyes. You shall write them on the doorposts of your house and on your gates.*

The primary concern of families in Old Testament times was nurturing covenant loyalty in the relationship with God among coming generations. Deuteronomy 6 offers an incisive challenge to godly parents about leading their children into a long-term relationship with the Lord. So this third taste of the D6 pie shifts the covenant focus ahead so that it lasts through time.

First Generation Nurturing

What Moses has already touched on in Deuteronomy (see 4:9-10, 25, 40; 5:9-10, 29) now takes center stage. The present generation of God's people must do all they possibly can to instill covenant loyalty within the coming generations. A relationship with the Lord must continue as our children come to know Him.

In order for this transfer to happen, though, God must instruct parents in the finer points of what loyalty in the relationship means. Six features outline this process, according to the sixth verse.

Number one is the content of what God's covenant partners must know: "these words." While this phrase speaks primarily of the *Shema* and the Great Commandment in verses 4 and 5, no doubt it also reaches back to describe everything God has revealed thus far about His covenants and promises to Israel since He first revealed His will to Abraham. The Lord's people must know in their mind and by their experience the **revealed truth** God has given them.

A second feature of God's instruction is the **pressing obligation** upon His covenant people. What He has told them is mandatory; He commands them to be loyal in the relationship. Notice, third, that the Lord Himself ("I") is the **experienced teacher** here and, fourth, that He expects His people ("you") to be **receptive learners.**

Fifth, the learning process offers a **continuing relevance.** It is always new and fresh because there are unexplored dimensions of covenant loyalty and blessing in the relationship just awaiting the people of God with every new experience. And while the teaching must work itself out on the proving ground of life, it originates in the heart: "these words . . . shall be on your heart." The great truths about God, His promises, covenant, and redemption must saturate and shape the **conscious reflection** of His people so that they live and breathe loyalty to the God they know.

Second Generation Nurturing

Only when fathers and mothers love God with a loyal heart (verses 4 and 5) can they turn their focus on helping their children cultivate such a relationship. We cannot give what we do not have. Yet once the truth of God grips our hearts and governs our lives, it can't stay just with us. It must work through us to shape and influence those we love the most.

What to Do

Verse 7 reminds us that these great words must shape our families. So "teach them diligently," Moses commands. The single Hebrew verb translated "teach diligently" pictures inscribing words into stone with great care and precision and keeping it up until the job is done.

How to Do It

While the example we set before our children is critical, we must teach intentionally with our words. "Talk of them"—that is, deliberately bring God into your conversations. In planned devotional times, in casual remarks, in simply talking about life, let what you're saying reinforce what you're trying to live before your children.

> In planned devotional times, in casual remarks, in simply talking about life, let what you're saying reinforce what you're trying to live before your children.

When verses 8 and 9 speak of "binding" these words on your hands, setting them before your eyes, and writing them on the doorposts and gates of your house, this is a powerful way of saying that your life, your home, and everything about you should boldly display your relationship with God. Many Jewish people take this counsel literally by wearing phylacteries—armbands and headbands with small compartments containing the covenant words—and displaying *mezuzot* (parchments incribed with verses from Deuteronomy 6 and 11) on their doors, but the point is that if these words are really "on our hearts" they will also be in our lives.

With Whom to Do It

Our first priority is sharing our faith with our children. Sons and daughters represent gracious gifts of God's favor. While they are certainly His heritage (see Psalm 127:3-5; 128:3-4; and Proverbs 17:6), children are born with sinful natures and need redemption. Parents who love their children will do everything in their power to lead them to a covenant relationship with the God who has provided salvation for them.

When to Do It

Our relationship with God must form our lifestyle. Therefore we are always teaching: as Moses says, when we sit, walk, lie down, and get up (verse 7). That's how we live. It's who we are. God's presence at the center of our lives means He will make a difference everywhere else in our lives. In Old Testament days, mothers taught their daughters the ways of the Lord as they taught them how to cook and sew. Plowing, harvesting, tending to livestock, and other duties of the men in the family provided a time for fathers to teach their sons the Torah. Children saw firsthand what a relationship with God looks like when their parents saw all of life as an opportunity to teach.

God's presence at the center of our lives means He will make a difference everywhere else in our lives.

4. WE TREASURE THE RELATIONSHIP:

The beauty of life flourishes in the blessing of God (Deuteronomy 6:10-15)

> *And when the Lord your God brings you into the land that he swore to your fathers, to Abraham,*

to Isaac, and to Jacob, to give you—with great and good cities that you did not build, and houses full of all good things that you did not fill, and cisterns that you did not dig, and vineyards and olive trees that you did not plant—and when you eat and are full, then take care lest you forget the LORD, who brought you out of the land of Egypt, out of the house of slavery. It is the LORD your God you shall fear. Him you shall serve and by his name you shall swear. You shall not go after other gods, the gods of the peoples who are around you, for the LORD your God in your midst is a jealous God, lest the anger of the LORD your God be kindled against you, and he destroy you from off the face of the earth.

Shaping the next generation in their walk with God doesn't happen just because we are proactive parents. Our children will come to love God because He is true to His promises. A godly family happens because the Lord graciously blesses His people. Try the fourth bite of the pie.

God is Faithful to His Own Character

Covenant loyalty is two-sided. It first flows out of God's faithfulness to Himself. He keeps His word because He is righteous. As verse 10 begins, we note the relationship that is already in place: "The LORD your God." His people enter the land because He had promised Abraham, Isaac, and Jacob that He would give it to them and to their children. Remember that land in the Old Testament speaks to us of God's provision of life.

All of the opportunities to show Him faithfulness are gifts of His grace. He "gives" the land to His people (v. 10), and with it come cities they did not build, houses they did not fill, cisterns they did not dig, and crops they did not plant. The danger they then faced is the one we deal with as well: taking God's generous grace lightly. We must recognize that a life of covenant loyalty is a full life packed with rich blessings. Yet we have earned none of these good things. And any degree of success we may see in nurturing a family for God is not a reward for our effort. It is a gift. It is His blessing through grace.

So when your children are redeemed, grounded in holy living, making good choices, and living in God's will, it's not because you are a gifted parent. It's because He is a great God.

Any degree of success we may see in nurturing a family for God is not a reward for our effort. It is a gift.

God is Faithful to His Faithful People

While the Lord always does His part in the relationship, we are the x-factor. "Take care," He says, to be faithful. How can we expect our children to trust God if our claim to know Him is nothing but an empty echo ringing through a hollow life? Our text mentions three factors of faithfulness.

Do Not Forget God

In many places Deuteronomy reminds us to "remember" our loyalty to God. Verse 12 in chapter 6 cautions us to "take care lest you forget the LORD." It's not that the knowledge of God will just slip out of our minds. No, remembering or "not forgetting" means believing and living in such a way that there is no question He is our God. How can we "forget" the Redeemer who rescued us from our bondage?

Do Not Follow Other Gods

The directive in verse 14 about giving God singular worship was quite the counter-cultural challenge in Moses' day as it is in ours. The reality was and still is that many options for worship present themselves to people. Yet all of the other "gods" in a pluralistic society are mere extensions of creation, of human nature, and are false in their offer to deliver ultimate truth and meaning.

The Lord alone is the transcendent Creator who is truth. Only He makes sense of how all things came to be, what they mean, and why they have moral implications. In this way, He is "jealous," according to verse 15. The fact that God is jealous does not mean that He expresses the sinful desire we experience as "jealousy," but that He rightly insists that our relationship with Him be an exclusive one. Only in knowing Him do we have life, blessings, and peace. He doesn't want us to miss out on these. To leave this God is to leave life and to find only ruin, destruction, and death.

Fear God

At the center of loyalty as in the chapter itself (see vv. 2 and 24) stands the fear of God. Literally verse 13 opens, "the LORD your God you shall fear." The reminder of the relationship comes first: He is the LORD—His covenant name—and He is our God. Moses goes on in this verse to define that trusting relationship by two effects it produces: "Him you shall serve and by his name you shall swear." The word translated "serve" shares its root with the term for "slavery" noted just above in verse 12 regarding Egyptian bondage. A covenant bond with Yahweh transforms cruel oppression into fruitful opportunity.

"Swearing" by the Lord's name here carries the idea of pledging allegiance to the true God. Our promise to be loyal to Him reflects the highest devotion, the ultimate commitment to a God who is always true to Himself and to His word. If this verse sounds familiar, it should since Jesus Himself quoted it when the devil tested His loyalty (Matthew 4:10).

Our children need to know that the best life, the life God blesses, is the one which keeps nothing from Him and receives everything through Him.

Our children need to know that the best life, the life God blesses, is the one which keeps nothing from Him and receives everything through Him.

5. WE MAINTAIN THE RELATIONSHIP:

The goal of life is staying loyal to God (Deuteronomy 6:16-19)

You shall not put the L*ORD your God to the test, as you tested him at Massah. You shall diligently keep the commandments of the* L*ORD your God,* *and his testimonies and his statutes, which he has commanded you. And you shall do what is right and good in the sight of the LORD, that it may go well with you, and that you may go in and take possession of the good land that the LORD swore to give to your fathers by thrusting out all your enemies from before you, as the LORD has promised.*

It's one thing to begin a relationship with the white-hot passion of brand new, fresh commitment. The tough part, though, is staying true down through the years as the initial surge of devotion retreats. We must not turn down the excitement but turn the excitement into renewed commitment that sees each day as a chance to fear and love God. Verses 16-19, the fifth bite of the pie, offer three strategies for daily loyalty to God.

Trust the Lord

Much of Israel's history was spent testing God as they had done at Massah, a place in the wilderness whose name means "testing" (v. 16). Testing is the opposite of trusting. We test God when we really aren't sure if we believe He will do what He says He will do. In Matthew 4:7, when Satan challenged Jesus to throw Himself off the temple, Jesus cites Deuteronomy 6:16 to counter the devil's test.

> Trust lies at the heart of a relationship with God. It's always been that way.

Trust lies at the heart of a relationship with God. It's always been that way. Believing God enough to commit one's life to Him makes a person right with God, as it did Abraham (Genesis 15:6). At critical junctures in the history of God's people up until Deuteronomy 6 their faith or the lack of it has made all the difference (see Exodus 4:31; 14:31; 19:9; Numbers 5:6; 14:11; 20:12; Deuteronomy 1:32). What was true then is still true now. If we, our children, and their children are to stay true to the Lord, we will do so only by continuing to trust Him.

Obey the Lord

A believing heart prompts a mom, dad, or child to "diligently keep" God's commandments (v. 17). That means doing what is "right and good," according to verse 18. We do "right" when we make choices in life which reflect the character of the God we love. The standard for what is right is the Lord Himself, not what we think, what our friends think, or what our culture thinks. And when the way we live satisfies our deepest needs and reflects what God desires, we know something of what it means to "do good."

Families committed to a covenant relationship with God will do their best day in and day out to live a life pleasing "in the eyes of the LORD." What He thinks of us will matter more than any other standard of so-called "success" our culture tries to pawn off on us.

Enjoy the Lord

Verse 18 makes it clear when we do what is good before God by trusting and obeying Him, He will do good for us. It will "go well with" His people who are faithful in the relationship.

In a word play, the Hebrew says literally, "It will be good for you" in the "good" land God is giving them.

The basis for enjoying life in God is the assured fact He is loyal to His promise. He keeps His word. Once more Moses tells us this by means of another pun to capture our attention. In verse 13 he insists we "swear" by the Lord's name. Then he later explains in verse 18 when we are loyal, Yahweh will do good for us because He Himself "swore" to do that very thing. You be loyal because He is loyal! He has proven it by doing exactly what He said (v. 19).

6. WE IMPART THE RELATIONSHIP:

The hope of life is sharing the grace of God (Deuteronomy 6:20-25)

> *When your son asks you in time to come, "What is the meaning of the testimonies and the statutes and the rules that the LORD our God has commanded you?" then you shall say to your son, "We were Pharaoh's slaves in Egypt. And the LORD brought us out of Egypt with a mighty hand. And the LORD showed signs and wonders, great and grievous, against Egypt and against Pharaoh and all his household, before our eyes. And he brought us out from there, that he might bring us in and give us the land that he swore to give to our fathers. And the LORD commanded us to do all these statutes, to fear the LORD our God, for our good always, that he might preserve us alive, as*

we are this day. And it will be righteousness for us, if we are careful to do all this commandment before the LORD our God, as he has commanded us."

It's easy for us to overlook the past. The demands of today seem so urgent and the complexities of tomorrow press us sooner than we think. But each new day bears the mark of choices we made yesterday and the day before and back and back—who knows how far? Every feature of our lives both right now and tomorrow is the product of countless decisions of the past, and not one of them catches God by surprise. What we do today impacts how our children will live tomorrow. Moses anticipates that and looks ahead. Here is the sixth bite of the D6 pie.

> What we do today impacts how our children will live tomorrow.

THE QUESTION OF TOMORROW

One day, one tomorrow, as you are pasturing the herd or heading to Jerusalem for the Sukkoth festival, your son will ask you a question, Moses predicts. He will wonder, "Dad, why do you keep all of these laws and traditions? What are they all about? What do they mean?" (v. 20). *Here, in the context of life's greatest loyalty and most important relationship, a son asks his father the most critical question of life: "Tell me about this God of ours and what He expects from me."* Whether you realize it or not, your children have wondered or will wonder the same thing. You need to know the answer when they ask.

Several encouraging assumptions become evident when this question arises. The son speaks of "the LORD *our* God" (verse 20), inferring that he views Yahweh as his God as well as the God of his parents. At least to some extent, he has already embraced a relationship with the family's covenant Lord.

Then, too, the fact that he would ask his father this question presumes that his dad is himself still loyal to God. The boy thinks it appropriate to ask him such an important question; he sees his father as worthy to give him an answer. Of course this scenario also implies that the children can see the parent's covenant loyalty. Their parents' lives are witnesses to a genuine, vital relationship with Yahweh, so much so that their children naturally bring up the subject.

Also encouraging is the premise that this son wants to know what it means to be faithful to God. He is interested enough to ask. What's more, he assumes that his father can give him a correct answer. He knows enough of his family's worship experience to be confident that their devotion is true and that it holds answers for him.

The bottom line is that these parents have lived such a loyal life committed to God that their children have taken notice and are interested in following that example.

The Answer for Today

Now comes the father's answer to his son's question. It offers the most important information a parent can give his child because it's all about how to know God.

It Begins with Redemption

The answer zeroes in on where we used to be and what God has done for us. "We were Pharaoh's slaves in Egypt," begins the story (v. 21). Bound to an idolatrous culture of sin, Israel had languished without hope for over four centuries. Without hope, that is, except for the Lord's promise to Abraham that must have seemed far out of reach in Egypt.

But God had not forgotten. He "brought us out of Egypt with a mighty hand," recounts the father. That great deliverance from bondage is *the* Old Testament redemption. Twenty-six of the 39 books mention it. God's "mighty hand" redeemed His people. Children need to know how powerful God's hand is when He saves us. And this entire story is true! God did it in public, in full view of everyone, confirming His power with signs and wonders. Verse 23 repeats this great truth: "God brought us out! He delivered us, and we were out of there!"

> Children need to know how powerful God's hand is when He saves us.

It Continues with Relationship

God brought us *out*, the father continues, so that He could bring us *in* (v. 23). He brings us into the land, into life, into abundance, into the satisfaction of knowing Him as our God. When we come to know God, we enter peace, blessing, fulfillment, security, salvation, and provision. In short, we find life. As verse 24 says literally, "he lets us live."

In return, since a covenant is a two-way pledge, the Lord expects us to be loyal. Once more our faithfulness expresses the fact that we "fear" Him. Remember, "fearing God" is the main Old Testament description for a genuine relationship of trusting obedience. As we trust, obey, and fear Him, we receive His "righteousness" (v. 25). We stand "right" before him not because we work for it or have somehow earned it, but because we trust Him to provide it for us.

In the deepest part of all that we are, we must love God.

So the "tomorrow" of verse 20 has become "this day" of verse 24. A father has answered his son's question about the most important thing in life. We now come full circle to end as we began, talking about the center, the axis, the one truth that holds life together. Once more, it is "this commandment," the Great Commandment: "Love the LORD your God with all your heart and with all your soul and with all your might." That's what matters most.

D6 DNA: THE THREAD

Where Deuteronomy 6 leads in scripture

D6 presents parents two compelling challenges. In the deepest part of all that we are, we must love God. That's home ground, job one, prime tasking. Coupled with our love for God is the second challenge: loving those closest to us into a place where they, too, can enjoy His love. This "double helix" of D6's DNA extends across the entire breadth of the Bible's message. It really is the language of life for people facing death.

God alone

The Old Testament is relentless in this reminder to us that God is the most important person in the universe and that the top concern of our lives must be to know Him personally. The first commandment of the ten insists that no one or nothing else deserves first place in our lives (Exodus 20:3; Deuteronomy 5:7). Despite losing just about everything he had, Job testified that God was really everything to him (Job 1:21). Joshua challenged the people about to enter Canaan to show total commitment to Yahweh in an exclusive covenant relationship (24:14-15, 23).

Psalms and Proverbs add their voices to this appeal as well. David's spirit was desperate for God alone (Psalm 63:1-3), and in Psalm 86:11, he prayed that God would give him an undivided heart totally devoted to the fear of the Lord. Moses knew that God's covenant love would satisfy him (Psalm 90:14). "Trust in the LORD with all your heart," counsels Solomon as well (Proverbs 3:5).

So, too, say the Old Testament prophets. "Turn to me and be saved, all the ends of the earth! For I am God, and there is no other," pleads Isaiah (45:22). His contemporary, Micah, concludes that God simply requires that we "walk humbly" with Him in a loyal covenant relationship (Micah 6:6-8). One hundred years later, Habakkuk resolves that despite no blossoming fig trees, no fruitful vines, and no cattle in the stalls, he would rejoice in the Lord (3:17-18). His God was everything to Him.

The fear factor

Also at the heart of the Old Testament, remember, is the fear of the Lord, the standard description of a covenant relationship with God. Fearing God brings us stability and satisfaction (Isaiah 33:6) and ultimately is life itself (Proverbs 14:27; 19:23). It is the prerequisite for knowing how to live wisely (Job 28:28; Proverbs 1:7; 9:10). According to Qoheleth, the fear of the Lord is the most vital concern in a person's life (Ecclesiastes 12:13).

This all-consuming love for God so prominent in the Old Testament arches over into the New as well, yet with one massive difference. Because of Jesus' coming, our devotion to God the Father is expressed to Him through Jesus His Son. What the Old Testament attributes to Yahweh, "the LORD," the New Testament attributes to Jesus (see, for example, Isaiah 40:3 with Matthew 3:3; Isaiah 8:13 with 1 Peter 3:15; Psalm 97:7 with Hebrews 1:6; Joel 2:32 with Romans 10:13). To love God supremely is to love Jesus supremely.

> To love God supremely is to love Jesus supremely.

Realize, then, even love for our family should not stand in the way of our love for Christ (Matthew 10:37-39; Luke 14:26-27). If we gain everything in the world yet reject Jesus, we really lose everything (Matthew 16:24-26). If we miss knowing God through Jesus, we miss life itself (John 17:3).

Here we should note especially the connection between Jesus and Deuteronomy 6. He makes it crystal clear the primal command to love God with all our being still applies to people under the New Covenant. An expert in Jewish law once tried to put Jesus on the spot. He questioned the Lord about which of the 613 laws in the Old Testament was the most important one. Without hesitation, Christ replied, "You shall love the Lord your God with all your heart and with all your soul and with all your mind. This is the great and first commandment" (Matthew 22:34-40; Mark 12:28-31; Luke 10:25-28).

Paul, too, tells us just how vital a relationship with Christ really is. I'm not even the one living, he insists, but it's Christ who is alive in me (Galatians 2:20). For Paul, "to live is Christ" (Philippians 1:21); everything else is loss next to the most important thing in the world—and that's knowing Jesus as Lord (Philippians 3:8). The ultimate privilege and supreme joy of our existence is this grace-given, faith-forged connection with God through Jesus that gives us life to the absolute max.

D6 in all 66

Since that's the case, the mandate Moses gives in Deuteronomy 6 to teach our children to learn and love God reverberates throughout the Bible. As early as Genesis 18:19 we learn that Abraham will teach his children the way of the Lord. Exodus 12:26 and 13:14 offer what must be one of the first examples of how a father tells his son the story of redemption. God instructs His people to read the Torah to the "little ones" so they will learn to fear Him (Deuteronomy 31:10-13). How crucial these times of teaching are since the truths God reveals in His Word belong especially to us and to our children forever (Deuteronomy 29:29).

The mandate Moses gives in Deuteronomy 6 to teach our children to learn and love God reverberates throughout the Bible.

The D6 mandate continues through the time of Israel's settlement in the Promised Land and during the kingdom period. According to Joshua 4:6, 20-24, Israelite dads were to pass along to their sons the stories of God's great deeds in leading them to the land. Even though his father worshiped Baal, Gideon had heard tales of these great exploits passed along through his family (Judges 6:13).

To every generation

Outside the five books of Moses, Psalms and Proverbs provide the most detailed look in the Old Testament at how parents should nurture their children in covenant life. Psalm 78 is a teaching psalm designed to instruct children in their covenant heritage. Verses 1 through 8 hit the note hard:

> *We will not hide them* [the things our fathers have told us] *from our children, but tell to the coming generation the glorious deeds of the Lord . . . He commanded our fathers to teach their children, that the next generation might know them, the children yet unborn, and arise and tell them to their children.*

Psalm 48:12-14 echoes this privilege parents have of telling the next generation about the glories of Christ's kingdom. "A people yet unborn" must hear of Messiah's great sacrifice (Psalm 22:30-31). And of course, one of a grandparent's joys is to delight

> Solomon's purpose is to give counsel to young people about how to live with good sense and with "God-sense."

the grandchildren with stories about God's unmatched power (Psalm 71:17-18; see also Psalm 44:1; 90:16-17).

The book of Proverbs interfaces with these nuggets of wisdom in Psalms. What results is a remarkably candid remix of Deuteronomy 6 challenging families to be faithful in their covenant with God. Solomon's purpose in this work is to give counsel to young people about how to live with good sense and with "God-sense."

Listen, my son

Echoing Deuteronomy 6, chapters 1-9 of Proverbs offer 10 teaching points designed to transform flabby parenting into focused parenting. Solomon expresses his counsel like a parent talking to his child, with each point beginning, "my son." We catch something of a father's heart and a mother's spirit as they plead with their kids to live for God. In the first teaching point, dad urges his boy to say "no" to the crowd when they try to pull him down (1:8-19).

In point two, the father challenges his son to "go for it" in living wisely (2:1-22), then follows up with a moving reminder to trust the Lord (3:1-12). Don't lose sight of the Lord's best for your life, urge the young man's parents in 3:15-25. Remember, too, they say, all that your family has taught you (4:1-9). The last five teaching points deal with such issues as avoiding paths that lead to death (4:10-19); guarding the heart (4:20-27); detecting and navigating around sex-baited traps (5:1-23; 6:20-7:27); staying out of debt and getting into good work habits (6:1-19). With all this counsel, wise D6 parents aim to guide their families confident that what God says is true.

> Wise D6 parents aim to guide their families confident that what God says is true.

Home-grown

God's concern for families who will love Him with all their being reaches into the New Testament as well. Young people honor their parents as they obey the Lord. Fathers must do their best to bring up children through discipline that teaches them how to live godly (Ephesians 6:1-4). In Colossians 3:20-21, Paul reinforces these parental duties with the added caution to dads not to go so far in their demands that they discourage their kids. Timothy's mother Eunice and grandmother Lois led him to faith. No doubt their example of loyal trust in Christ as well as their patient, consistent teaching convinced him the Bible's claims were true (2 Timothy 1:5; 3:14-16).

Families in the church on Crete under Titus' ministry modeled by word and lifestyle the spiritual disciplines which nourish faith. Those mature men and women lived Christ before their young people so the church reaped a harvest of disciples through seeds planted in the home (Titus 2:1-6).

Nothing matters more

Finally, one incredibly important text links the Old and New Testament concern for families that love and live God.

The passage is Malachi 2:10-16. This final book of the Minor Prophets and of the Old Covenant in our English Bibles focuses on the crucial theme of the covenant—how our covenant relationship with God shapes our relationships with others, particularly our families.

God's people have broken their covenant with Him, the prophet charges, and as a result are at odds with each other as well (2:10-11). They had abandoned the Lord despite Malachi's two reminders of what God had said earlier in Deuteronomy 6. The first D6 marker in Malachi 2 is the four-fold use of the word "one." Recall the great confession in the *Shema* that "the LORD (is) our God; the LORD is one" (Deuteronomy 6:4). God is absolutely preeminent. No one or nothing stands above Him; so it is in fact, and so it must be in our lives.

> Love the Lord your God with everything you have, and then do all in your power to cultivate that same love in your children.

Now Malachi emphasizes this unique place of our God once again. He is one Father and one Creator (2:10). And in bringing husband and wife together in covenant marriage, he makes their union unique, singular—"one" through His Spirit binding them in unity with each other and with Him (2:15).

So what was God's purpose in creating the man and the woman and joining them with Himself in a covenant union? What was the "one God" seeking, asks the prophet (2:15).

When we ask that question, we are pointing to nothing less than one of the most vital priorities of life itself, to the great wheel that keeps civilization turning and bends it in the direction of bringing supreme glory and honor to God Himself.

The answer—one of the great dynamics in the life of people linked in covenant with the living God—is godly children (2:15). The Lord of the covenant brings a man and a woman together under the authority of His word, consumed by the passion of His love, to present before Him children who also will love Him more than they love anything or anyone else. This will only happen, though, when a mom and a dad are totally devoted to God (2:16) and to each other (2:15-16). Here is the second marker directing us back to D6. Love the Lord your God with everything you have, and then do all in your power to cultivate that same love in your children.

Nothing in life—this life or the next—matters more.

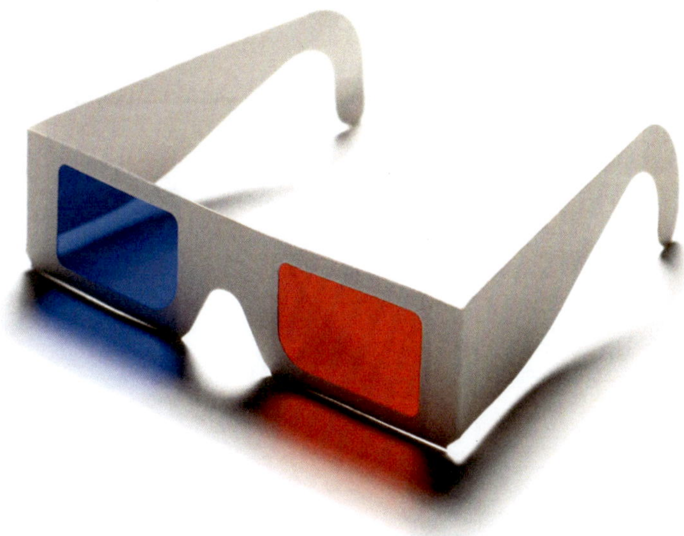

D6 DYNAMICS: THE TEACHING

How D6 looks in life

Unless Deuteronomy 6 and its profound message break into our lives and work their way into our affections to the point we want what God wants for our families, they remain just words on the page—curious, but not compelling; admirable, but with no authority. Here are six suggestions to make D6 come alive in our homes.

Start somewhere, and the best place is with God

I know some parents reading these words are saying something like, "As complex as life is today, answers like these aren't that simple. There can't be one key to life. That sounds too much like a cheesy late night cable TV infomercial preacher peddling his book on *The Secret to Power in Living* or *The Key to Successful Parenting*." Believe me, they have told me this very thing. But I'm not so sure they're right. Yes, life is messy and life is complicated. But one of the ways to deal with the mess is to simplify wherever we can—and we can in this matter of our devotion to God. If we get that right, if our relationship with Him is what it needs to be, the tidying up in other places will begin, too.

Love by raising the bar

Get "love" straight. Our chic parenting culture has turned "love" into one unchecked catering session where we think we are loving our children by giving them everything they want. But love is sometimes just raising the bar for them, not buying them the gym! Remember, God can *command* love. It may be that the best thing we can give our kids—the best way we can love them—is by setting a higher standard and letting them have no doubts that we think they can reach it. Then hold them to it. Sure, we will be there for them no matter what, and they need to know that. But love them enough to make reasonable requirements; don't just soft-peddle parenting as nothing more than a buddy-buddy, "I want you to have what I didn't" gift-giving fest.

> Love is sometimes just raising the bar for your children, not buying them the gym!

Love your children into the arms of Jesus

Do your best to influence your children to trust Christ when they are ready. That doesn't mean pushing them, but gently nudging them in a way that lets them know you care. My Mom did that with me. She told me stories of Jesus, made sure I understood what He did for me, and with a mother's touch, loved me to Christ. Love the Gospel, Mom and Dad. Be sure your children see Jesus not as a bully who orders us to go to church and be good, but as a refuge who calls us to everything that is good.

Recognize that little things always matter

When you live consistently for God, you impact your family more than you know—especially in the little things. They will tell you in years to come how one compliment you gave, one promise you kept, one sin you confessed made them respect you and proved to them that you really do walk with the Lord. Like me, you probably won't even remember that small detail. But your kids will. Teaching moments happen every day all around us and we never know it at the time. That's why we must be faithful, humble, and transparent.

> Teaching moments happen every day all around us and we never know it at the time.

Changing tires—bend to meet your children where they are

While the truth of God's Word is settled and absolute, you'd better be flexible and adaptable in how you respond to your children. Know their unique personalities, how and how not to confront, how and how not to encourage, when to forgive and when to enforce.

Not long after I turned 16 when Carol and I were dating, we were out on the town one night in my dad's 1969 brown Buick Skylark. We had parked along a side street while we enjoyed dinner at a restaurant. As we got back into the car and started to pull away, I realized something was wrong. Uh oh, flat tire! Even though my father had taught me how to change a flat, I was a bit unsure of myself, and I sure didn't want to blow the repair since my date was with me. So, since this was back in the day, I found a nearby phone booth and—no, I didn't change into my Superman costume—I called my dad, mostly for a bit of assurance.

His reply was short: "Well, son, you know what to do. Fix it." And he hung up. So I set about it. I did everything he had taught me, finished up, got back into the car, and we started to leave. Just then I noticed a familiar vehicle not far down the street turn on its lights and make its way slowly toward us. It was my dad in my mom's car. He had driven to where we were and had watched me toil and slave through most of the ordeal. He pulled next to us, rolled down his window, and said very matter-of-factly, "You did a good job, son," and pulled off into the night. At first I was furious! Why hadn't he helped me? But I realized he knew I would have been embarrassed to have my dad come and bail me out with something as simple as changing a flat. But he did want me to know he was there in case I had needed him. And frankly, once it was over, I was so relieved to know he had been there. Parents sometimes need to do search and rescue. Other times they just need to stay by the phone should it ring.

Make your address God's address

Make the spiritual seem natural in your home. Practice the spiritual disciplines—pray, read the Bible, sing, serve, testify, be active in church—and do it all with as much joy as you can! Make things of God part of conversations. Remember, as A. W. Tozer reminds us, "worship is the normal enjoyment of human beings." Keep God-honoring stories and traditions from the past alive in your house. Speak of God as a person, not just an idea, and expect to see Him at your table, through your tears, and in the smiles of your children. He'll be there.

Your family is a stewardship gift, a trust, and the greatest opportunity you'll have in this life to honor the God who gave them to you.

Make the spiritual seem natural in your home.

For more D6 information visit D6Family.com